D1257735

Poetry In Motion

By Nadir Rasheed

Introduction

I have always enjoyed written and verbal expression. From my youth, to my present age of 47, I have always put my thoughts, experiences and journeys on paper. This book is a compilation of my internal and external expressions. This book **is not** intended to **shape** your thinking. It is only intended to **get you to think**.

Life is like poetry. It has many styles, messages and dimensions. Poetry, like life, can be happy, sad, serious, comical, etc. Like life, poetry is action, motion and movement.

Time never stands still. Every **second** of our day is **moving** toward a predestined journey. This journey is **POETRY IN MOTION**.

Copyright Registration: TXU1-608-530

ISBN: 978-0-9794176-4-1

Acknowledgments

I give all praise and thanks to the **TRUE AUTHOR** (Allah, Yahweh, Jehovah, God, etc.). I would like to thank and honor my ex-wife Kim and my beautiful children Shenique, Kadre' and Khalil. Your love and support inspires me, daily.

I would like to thank my parents James (May you rest in peace) and Betty Ward for the love and wisdom they have given me throughout my life. You definitely laid a strong foundation. I am the way I am because of you. I thank my brothers Cedric and Chad Ward for all of the childhood memories and for the "present bond" that can never be broken. My brother, Cedric, is the creator and mastermind behind the cover of this book. There are many visionaries that could benefit from his creativity.

I would like to thank Amy Ward (Grandmother Amy – May you rest in peace) for her humor and "strict adherence" to the English language. You were definitely the life of every function. To Gabriella Hatcher (Grandmother Gay), may you rest in peace and always know that a part of you still LIVES in me.

Last, but not least, I would like to thank **North Smithfield Manor/Green Leaf Heights (THE VILLAGE that help raise me)**, all of my family, friends, colleagues, etc. There are so many of you that I would have to write another book to acknowledge all of you. I love you all. **I dedicate this book to Humanity**

Table of Contents

Table of Contents (Cont'd)

ARE YOU FREE?

In this life, you can be whatever you want to be
All you have to do is make up your mind
Every morning I wake up striving to be free
Because freedom is what I'm always searching to find
Everyone's definition of freedom is not the same
Some see freedom as being able to walk outside
Others see freedom as being able to change their name
While some see freedom as getting in the car and going for a
ride

Many of us see freedom as being removed from debt
While others see freedom as expressions of the voice
Some see freedom as not having any regrets
As others see freedom as being able to make a choice
If your **mind** is free, the battle of life is half-won
Please don't take this freedom for granted
Because the quest for freedom is a race we must run
Through the gardens of the seeds we've planted
My prayer is that **everyone in the world** becomes free
Free from the dependencies of things that cause us harm

Freedom from stress

Freedom from anger

Freedom from jealousy

And above all, freedom from self-destruction! **Are you free?**

"Why"

We all have eyes but we all don't see

We all have ears but we all don't hear

We all have mouths but we all don't speak

We all have hearts but we all don't feel

Why is that?

I SEE LOVE

When I look into your eyes, I see love

When I look into your heart, I see love

When I think about your thoughts, I see love

When I'm blessed with your presence, I see love

In a world filled with so much hate

People's emotions filled with envy and greed

Hatred is an emotion that's hard for me to relate

A sad reality as I watch my Brothers and Sisters of Humanity
bleed

When I look into the Heavens, I see love

When I look into the Oceans, I see love

In a world filled with so much hate

"Thank God", I see nothing but love

"The Answer"

When purity becomes diluted
The waters and fountains of Knowledge become polluted
As a humble man, I sit in the presence of anger
Watching non-tolerant people create environments of danger

We must embrace as one Humanity
While we erase and replace Un-Godly insanity
Indeed this will take 100% participation
That means partnering with those outside your congregation

I know these words will fall on many deaf ears
While you focus on hocus-pocus media images designed to
increase your fears
Many of you will look the other way because you don't care
Blind eyes will never see the tree or the fruit that it bears

When this life ends, our deeds will show our contribution
Some of us were part of the problem while others were part
of the solution
The seeds that bleed our society are spreading like Cancer
You've always had many questions, but now you've been
given The Answer

Love, Peace & Happiness

Love, Peace and Happiness – for these I pray
Sometimes I search for the words, but have nothing to say
Wisdom and Knowledge rattle through my brain
Frustrated by the system, but I won't complain

Driving by the Homeless, I feel so ashamed
To the wealthy Politicians, it's just a game
Feeding the Homeless Turkey and Dressing on a Holiday
You hypocrites, they need to eat **every day**

Taking money from the Poor while giving it to the Rich
I wonder how **you'd react** if the roles were switched
Smiling in their faces while stabbing them in the back
You can't fund Medicaid, but you can fund Iraq?

Love, Peace and Happiness – for these I pray
Sometimes I search for the words, but have nothing to say
Wisdom and Knowledge rattle through my brain
Frustrated by the system, but I won't complain

The Value of Family

There used to be a time when family was valued

A time when meals and conversation were shared at the
kitchen table

A time when the experience and wisdom of our elders
fascinated us

Even when times were tough, just knowing we had family
support made everything OK

What happen to those times?

There used to be a time when family was appreciated

A time when you had to be **in the house** before the street
lights came on

A time when everyone in the house watched a movie
together

Even if you didn't like the movie, you enjoyed the time spent
with your family

What happen to those times?

There used to be a time when family was honored

A time when men were the head of the house; not dictators,
but examples to be followed

A time when the man and woman of the house were
disciplinarian teachers

Even if you didn't like the lessons, you learned from their
tough love

What happen to those times?

In 2018, the foundation of the family structure has a crack in
it

The **F**ather is absent (Spiritually and Physically)

The **A**ttitudes of the children are disrespectful and shameful

The **M**other is now **both parents** (in body and role)

The **I**nterest in the family's history and heritage is gone

The **L**ove that should be present in and out of the home has
disappeared

The **YOU** that was part of the family is **now an individual**

The old African Proverb says: It takes a **whole village** to raise
a child

Has the village been burned?

Have the children run away (escaped) from the village?

Only the Kings and Queens of the village can answer **that**
question

Tears

Flowing waters from internal rain

External emotion from internal pain

Overjoyed happiness can cause tears to flow

Then there are times when we cry for reasons we just don't
know

Good-hearted people find it easier to cry

While hard-hearted people shed tears that they'll **always**
deny

Behind closed doors we face what's real

While in the public's eye, we personify a fictitious shield

Tears can be therapy to a battered soul

While tears can be a **prison** that keeps your life on hold

We all shed tears, this we can't deny

So deal with the **reasons** that cause you to cry

Embrace your tears!

PIMPS OF THE PULPIT

Pimps of the Pulpit
Benefiting while their Congregation's pockets are hit
Sharing **your** Tithes and Offerings with **their spouses**
Your Tithes and Offerings are financing **their new cars and houses**
Praying to God that you get a pay increase or a new career
That means the **Pimps of the Pulpit get RICHER every year**
Bring all your Tithes and Offerings into the Storehouse that there may be meat in **his**
Using the Book of Malachi to exploit your Godly fears
Barely able to pay your light bill and put food on your table – the **Congregation's life is hard**
The Pimps of the Pulpit tell you to pray, buy **their CD's and pay for it with your credit cards**
Pimps of the Pulpit – Millionaires creating a Spiritual Sensation
Climbing the steps of **financial wealth off the backs of their Congregations**
Did Abraham, Noah, Moses and Jesus benefit financially for teaching God's Word?
Pimps of the Pulpit should get wealthy off God's Word? That's absurd!!!!
Pimps of the Pulpit, **how do you sleep?**
Woe to the Pimps that scatter God's Sheep!!!!

"I Won't Quit"

Staring at the sunlight
My eyes are burning
I'm full of courage and fight
That's why my soul is yearning
For my success
That's my test
And I must confess
That I'm blessed
Because it's Voice penetrated the walls in my Chest
This Journey of mine isn't the Beginning
Nor is it the End
I get hit
But I won't quit
Until I win
I'm self-hired and inspired
By those who sacrificed before me
I'm not in it to be admired
For future success can no longer ignore me
When I make it to the top of the mountain
I won't forget the painful steps that it took
I will drink from this wealthy fountain
Rewriting my own history book
I can take a punch
I know, because I've been hit
My obstacles better "pack a lunch"
Because I Won't Quit

The Gift

God gives us all special gifts
Some spend a lifetime trying to find them
We sometimes realize them in low valleys and high cliffs
Even then, Satan tries to bind them

Whatever God has called you to do
It is your purpose in life, indeed
To your Gift is your purpose; so always be true
When the Gift is from God, it will ALWAYS succeed

As we search ourselves to find ourselves
Success is what we always measure
Like the knowledge in the books that brace our shelves
The Gift from God is our Treasure

Use the Gift or misuse the Gift
Because of God's Grace and Mercy, we have a choice
Through all days, I give praise and will truly lift
The Gift that God has placed in my voice

Written & Produced By: **Nadir F. Rasheed**
Dedicated to: **Kimberly Sims**

It's Never Too Late

Patient days breed impatient ways
Harmony breeds disharmony when you're confused by the
maze
Spiritual and lyrical manifestations have their place
In your heart; not by the fake expressions on your face

Disillusioned by what your eyes see
Confused by your soul's yearning desire to be free
Physically living but metaphorically dead
Many degrees on your wall, but no knowledge in your head

Before you can love others, you must love yourself
Morally bankrupt while you're searching for wealth
Don't' get upset if you can't relate
Get on the right path because it's never too late

Positive Outlook

Thinking about things we want; we sometimes complain
We can't appreciate the sun because we only analyze the rain
Searching the earth, from our birth, is an overdrawn
conclusion
Running away from the Light and toward Darkness and
confusion

When will we bathe in the waters of purity?
We constantly forsake safety but continue to beg for security
Complaining about our possessions that the world took
Stay away from the negative elements and keep a positive
outlook

PRAY vs. PREY

Pray vs. Prey
Which are **you** about?
It's not about what you **say**
It's your actions that leave **no doubt**

When you are weak, do you **pray**?
Or do you **prey** on the weak?
No matter what you **say**
Your **motives** show the path **you seek**

So you ask, what's the moral of this story?
It's not about what you **say**
Do you pray to seek **God's Glory**?
Or do you **prey on the weak** every day?

THINK 4 YOURSELF

Fantasy is what people want
Reality is what people need
Success and Failure create an Emotional taunt
Because of this, only conscious minds will succeed

But what is Success?
If your definition is **only** material, you missed it
Through life's test, you've been cursed and blessed
But which **moral** lesson does **your** mind forget?

All Spiritual and no Material has no balance
All Material and no Spiritual is the same
Thinking with **your own mind** is the challenge
Because you never learned the rules, how did you think you'd
win the game?

Since you got here, you were **given** your thoughts
This only **adds** to the confusion
When you **questioned** this thinking, you were rebuked
Now you're afraid to come to **your own conclusion**
My Advice: Think 4 Yourself and come out of the illusion

Switchin Places

What if the rich and the poor could switch places?
I'd be a fly on the wall to see the expression on their faces
The totality of their mentalities would seem strange
Now that their chances and circumstances have begun to
change

Now that you're on the other side, what do you see?
Would you still look at YOU like you now look at me?
What goes around, comes around, is a favorite saying
Now that you're on the OTHER side, you embrace praying

The poor and homeless are lazy; that's the stereotype
Now that YOU are poor and homeless, do YOU still believe in
the hype?
It doesn't matter about your status, gender, political
affiliation or races
We'd have a different perspective if we HAD to switch places

I'll Expose You

My lyrics are like spirits
You can't comprehend even though you hear it
The best poets fear it
The best reciters won't come near it
Shaking your thoughts with my lines
Busting the bricks in your mind
Giving you sight while I enlight
Although you can see, you're still blind
Keeping it shallow though it's deep
Keeping you awake while you're asleep
Like the wolves that slaughter the sheep
You always sow what you'll reap
Claiming it's Peace while you fight
Keeping your Darkness from Light
In spite, you continue your plight
You claim it's Day when it's Night
Got us divided by your names
For you and the Elite it's just a game
To the Ignorant Ones it's all the same
So you ask, who are we to blame?
I'll expose your plan to the masses
Regardless of status or classes
Like an inscription in a prescription
I'll adjust your sight like your glasses
I'll always obey the Law
Taking notes of everything I saw
I'm not frozen cause I'm chosen – Helping the rest of
humanity to unthaw – **I'll Expose You!**

The Lesson

Wake Up from the deep sleep of depression
You're taking your body, mind, heart and soul through a
recession
Stop going to the priest with your confession
You went to school all those years and never learned THE
LESSON

Your eyes are open, but your mind is asleep
THE LESSON is shallow, but damn it's so deep
Stop holding on to things that you weren't meant to keep
It's one's faith that states the case from which one must leap

Never look to society for the answer
Don't be fooled or schooled by the speaker or the dancer
Spiritual knowledge is its own college and enhancer
You DO KNOW that there IS a cure for Cancer?

Come out of the cave of darkness within your mind
Because of your 20/20 vision, you're convinced you're not
blind
The shake-up must wake up the treasures you couldn't find
THE LESSON – Faith with "Godly" work IS DIVINE

Women Overcome

I thank God for your grace
The pains of your struggles on your face
You're **the** asset of our race
Women Overcome

Loving us when we don't love ourselves
Educating us with the books on your shelves
Teaching us where **true** manhood dwells
Women Overcome

Even when you're frustrated with life
You remain the loving, loyal wife
Seeing your tears cut like a knife
Women Overcome

Without you we are nothing
Because of you we are something
Please remember this one thing –
Women Overcome

Through life's trials and tribulations, you never complain
We benefit from your bounty like the Earth benefits from rain
Oh what I'd do to take away all of your pain
Women Overcome

Will The Real People Please Stand Up!!!!

From the second to the minute to the hour of the month
I'm sick of fake educated people putting on a front
Got their heads up in the air as they brag about their degrees
They're just a mis-educated disease

Thinking they are where they are because of **who** they are
Forgetting that it was the **Creator** that brought them this far
It's only **God's Mercy** that saved them from their own
mishaps
But they tell the world that they pulled **themselves up** by
their **"own boot straps"**

Will the real people please stand up and give God the Glory
You don't have to make up any lies; just tell your story
You see, your knowledge and riches are **indeed "true wealth"**
When you understand that victory and success **never come
from yourself**

KEEP ON MOVIN

Sometimes life is difficult
It seems that the harder we try, the more difficult life gets
Just imagine how difficult life would be if we stop trying
BE PERSISTENT and **KEEP ON MOVIN**

Sometimes we get tired
It seems that it would be much easier to give up
Just imagine what life would be like if we always gave up
BE CONSISTENT and **KEEP ON MOVIN**

Sometimes we get scared
Afraid that our dreams are unreachable
Just imagine what life would be like without vision
BE COURAGEOUS and **KEEP ON MOVIN**

KEEP ON MOVIN!
KEEP ON MOVIN!
KEEP ON MOVIN!
For if we are **CONSTANTLY** in motion, **we will never have
time to stand still**

No One Can Stop Me But Me

I beat my Drum
Indeed I beat it Loud
My mothers' womb is where I come from **(AFRICA)**
Indeed I'm Confident and Proud
My life, a story of forty-seven years
My story-book is not complete
From the present, to the future, lie many fears
ALL NEGATIVES, **I WILL DEFEAT**
The **SYSTEM** tries to make things stressful
The **BLIND** system cannot see
That I **AM** going to be successful
BECAUSE ONLY I CAN STOP ME

AMEN!

Observation

As I walk through this **spacious earth**
I'm attracted to the **many miracles** I witness
Babies being born
Bees making honey
Birds flying with precision
The stars, moon and sun held **effortless** in the sky

As I observe the **signs of creation**
I'm attracted to the **perfection** of its construction
Humans having two eyes, but **one vision**
Two nostrils, but **one smell**
Two ears, but **one sound**
Two lips, but **one voice**
Two hands, but **one touch**

As I sit by the ocean
I'm attracted to the sound of **peace** caused by the waves
A **peace** that can **only** be appreciated through observation
Indeed, **observation** brings on **appreciation**

Learning To Share

To my brother, I give my hat
To my brother, I give my belt
To my brother, I give my shirt
To my brother, I also give my shoes

By giving you my hat, you may share my knowledge
By giving you my belt, you may share the support that holds
me up
By giving you my shirt, you may share my emotions
By giving you my shoes, you may also share my journey

For when we walk, talk and live together as ONE
We truly understand each other

Am I Still Dreamin?

I woke up from a **deep sleep**
I couldn't even think because my **nightmare** was too deep
I saw **brothers** killin **brothers**
And **babies** cursin-out their mothers
I'm glad it was just a dream

I saw **brothers** droppin out of school
Hangin and Slangin on the corner; thinkin it was cool
I wiped **tears** from their **mothers' eyes**
Tryin to erase the **tragedy of the Drive-Bys**
Man, I'm glad it was only a dream

Starved minds wouldn't eat; didn't wanna feed
Graduated from high school; **unable to read**
Young, **jobless brothers** drove the **fancy cars**
Only later to dwell in the home of the **prison bars**
Is this **reality** or **AM I STILL DREAMIN?**

A Silent Soul

Be Still My Soul, for you were created to **submit**
Be Still My Soul, for the troubles of life cannot contain thee
Be Still My Soul, for the wonders of **Creation** amaze thee

Be Still My Soul, for the body has **no life without thee**
Be Still My Soul, for you love to see others succeed
Be Still My Soul, and let time heal your wounds
For a **Silent Soul** is **always** at peace

"Brother Man"

"Brother Man" is a title that you can't take lightly
He's a father, a teacher, a man who corrects others politely
He's a humble brother even when he's on top
And when times get hard, you'll never see his head drop

To be a "Brother Man", you must respect your brother
That means respect mankind, and appreciate your Mother
You must respect the laws that govern the Land
And help someone else become a "Brother Man"

"Brother Man" gives life; he'll never take it
"Brother Man" is always real because his nature won't allow
him to fake it
"Brother Man" is overjoyed when his brothers succeed
And "Brother Man" is disappointed when his brothers make
each other bleed

Be a "Brother Man" for yourself
Be a "Brother Man" for others
Be a "Brother Man" for life
And if YOU can't be a "Brother Man", don't stand in the path
of those who can

"Sister Soldier"

A strong, positive woman is known as **"Sister Soldier"**
Some sisters possess this strength in their youth; others not
until they are much older
Out on the **Battlefield of Life**, you're a **hero**
Sometimes you get **100% acknowledgement**; sometimes you
get **zero**

Despite **many obstacles** you still press on
You **resurrect** the **strength** of your people that for ages has
been gone
Out on the **Battlefield of Life**, you **heal many wounds**
Hoping your **hard work** and **prayers** will bring the **VICTORY**
soon

"Sister Soldier", you **ignite** the torch that gives the Earth **light**
You raise negativity to positivity day and night
Out on the **Battlefield of Life**, you **nurture** us in our youth
and as we get older
March On! March On! March On! "Sister Soldier"

Who's To Say???

What if Down was Up

What if White was Black

What if a Glass was a Cup

What if the Front was the Back

"Who's To Say"???

What if a Glove was a Hat

What if Wine was Water

What if a Ball was a Bat

What if a Dime was a Quarter

"Who's To Say"???

What if a Shoe was a Rock

What if a Stroke was Cancer

What if a Watch was a Sock

What if a Question was an Answer

"Who's To Say"???

Follow Your Conscience

The Conscience has its own Judicial System
It convicts us when others have set us free
It places a burden that creates many sleepless nights
It shames us when others honor us

The Conscience has its own Voice
It speaks to the heart when the ears are not listening
It forces our eyes to open even when they are closed
It has a silent power that speaks loudly

The Conscience <u>ALWAYS</u> has a home
It lives in us; the people of the World
It <u>ALWAYS</u> gives us the intelligent answer
But the question is – DO WE FOLLOW IT?

Hidden Treasure

Walking through oceans that are dry; not wet
Traveling through deserts that are moist; not humid
Climbing over mountains that are short; not high
Out on a journey to find the **Hidden Treasure**

A Treasure that will make you **rich** for life
Never having to depend on the **material things** of the World
A Treasure that will make you humble; not arrogant
Never having to degrade others in order to feel strong

Looking for the **Hidden Treasure** in all of the wrong places
Later realizing you must be disciplined, patient, and wise
Once the **Hidden Treasure** is found, you're **truly amazed**
Because the **Treasure** has been there since the **Beginning**
(INSIDE OF YOU)!

Bring Them Up To Your Level

People seem to enjoy **ignorance**
So pretend to be ignorant and **give wise words**
People seem to enjoy **violence**
So fight their violence with **peace**
People seem to enjoy **hate**
So lure their hate into the **trap of love**
So, what's the **moral** of this story?
Don't lower yourself to **Society's** level
ELEVATE SOCIETY TO YOURS!

Hour Glass

I look at life through an **Hour Glass**
Watching the sand pass through the opening; extremely fast
The sands' movement reminds me of the **speed of life**
Several years ago I was married; now I have a daughter, two
sons and an Ex-Wife

Time is **precious** because it won't **stand still**
Don't think for a **minute** you've got **"time"** to kill
One day it's here and the next it's gone
Today you're surrounded by many; tomorrow you're all alone

Wake Up! **Time doesn't sleep**
Hold fast to the memories you choose to keep
Isn't it amazing how the **time has passed?**
You're looking at **Life** through an **Hour Glass**

Humbleness

Never believe that a dream is unreachable
Never believe that a mind is unteachable
Never believe that, toward others, you're superior
For when you think like this, **YOU** become inferior

Share your knowledge because **it's not YOURS**
Love, Peace and Happiness opens many doors
Never believe that, toward others, you're superior
For when you think like this, **YOU** become inferior

Share your wealth because **it's not YOURS**
Helping the **NEEDY** should be one of your chores
Never believe that, toward others, you're superior
For when you think like this, **YOU** become inferior

The Unlearned Song

If I was a Bird, I would fly
Fly – **high** above the problems of life
I would never worry about food, shelter or clothing
I would let Mans' ignorance be my nutrition
The Trees of the Earth would be my shelter
And my "God-given" feathers would be my clothing

If I was a Bird, I would whistle
Whistle – songs of peace for **ALL MANKIND**
Forcing man to acknowledge the **beauty** they encompass
I would wake man up **every morning** with a **Song** he has yet
to learn
Love, Peace and Happiness – this indeed is **The Unlearned
Song!**

Listen

Walk outside, close your eyes and listen
Listen to the sound of the peaceful breeze
Walk outside, close your eyes and listen
Listen to the chorus of the birds singing
Walk outside, close your eyes and listen
Listen to the rain as it feeds the earth
Walk outside, close your eyes and listen
And you will find there is **MUCH** to be heard

The Unknown

There's a storm, but no rain to cool the heat of hatred
There's a wind, but no breeze to blow away the roots of
injustice
There's a sun, but no light to shine on the evils in the dark
There's an education, but no knowledge on the reality of past
life
Where do these environmental traits lead?
The Earth thirsts for water, but from whose **WELL** shall it
come?
A **New Day** is coming, but who shall see it?
IS IT I?
IS IT I?
IS IT I?

Hate

Hate has no conscience
It exploits the weak and injures the harmless
Hate isn't a thought
It's a reaction to hidden fears, concerns and jealousies
Hate is a reality
It re-injures past wounds of society
Hate is **taught**
It is the element that is **reproduced from Generation to Generation**
Hate produces more hate
This is why Hate **will out-live us all**

Progressive Mind

Wake up with progress on your mind
Remove the negative thoughts you once held
Unlock the doors of vision and dreams
Make vision and dreams a part of your life

Wake up with an **open-mind**
Free from the distractions of tunnel vision
Unlock the doors of creativity
Make creativity your vehicle toward progress

Wake up with love on your mind
Free from the burdens of hate
Unlock the doors of love
Make love the **Garden** that **cultivates** your heart

Wake up with a Progressive mind
Wake up with an Open mind
Wake up with a Loving mind
And one day you will wake up with Success!

Man's So Smart He's Stupid

Through man's ignorance, birds are fed
Through man's wisdom, people are starving
What in the hell is going on?
How can a Millionaire live in a $20 million house, and neglect
the starving people of the world?
What in the hell is going on?
How can the President spend Billions of dollars to support
Wars, and neglect the starving people of the world?
What in the hell is going on?
If man is wise enough to go to the Moon, why is he foolish
enough to neglect the starving people of the world?
If man is wise enough to get a PH.D from Harvard, why is he
foolish enough to neglect the starving people of the world?
I'll tell you why!
Because man is wise in evil deeds and foolish in good deeds
In essence, **Man is so smart that he is stupid**
Smart enough to **see a need**, and too stupid to **satisfy it**

A Game of Symbols and Signs

The game of Baseball is more than you think!
It, like many other games, is a game full of symbols and signs
For those who see it as "just a game", that's all they see
But for those with knowledge of symbolism, it is much more
The game is played with a ball and a bat
The **Ball represents Truth** and the **Bat** is the **means of connecting to the Truth**
The **Field** (called a **Diamond = Priceless Jewel**) consists of **3 Bases and Home Plate**
First Base represents **Earth, Second Base** represents **Wind, Third Base** represents **Fire,** and **Home Plate** represents **Water** (that which gives **Life**)
The key players are the **Pitcher,** the **Hind-catcher,** and the **Batter**
The **Pitcher** and **Hind-catcher** represent those with **Elite Knowledge**
The **Batter represents** the **Common Man** with **General/Limited Knowledge**
The **Batter stands behind** Home Plate (**Water/Life**) which is **his Foundation**
The **Pitcher** throws the **Ball** (which represents **Truth**)
Through **Symbols and Signs,** the Hind-catcher communicates with the Pitcher
Keep in mind, the **Batter (Common Man) has no knowledge** of the Hind-catcher's **Symbols and Signs**
The Hind-catcher's goal is to give the Pitcher the **Symbol or Sign** that will make the **Batter (Common Man) miss** the Ball (**Truth**)
The Batter gets **Three** (A Divine Number since the Ancient Mysteries) chances to connect with the Ball (**Truth**)

Whenever the Batter hits the Ball, he exposes the "Common Man" to Knowledge known ONLY by the ELITE
Whenever the Batter (**Common Man**) hits a **Home Run**, he is granted **Free Passage around the Bases** (Earth, Wind, Fire and Water)
Each time the Batter misses the Ball (Truth), **it is a Strike toward his Passage into the Knowledge of the ELITE**
These are just a **few** of Baseball's **Symbols and Signs!**

The Pain of Hate

I feel the pain of hate rip through Society's bones
A life threatening disease that has yet to be cured
The wounds from hate date back to the beginning of time
Jealousy is the stimulant that intensifies its rage

I feel the pain of hate penetrate through Society's mind
A life threatening disease that runs through the streets like
the wind
The wounds from hate are hard to heal
Causing disturbances in innocent children who know nothing
but love

The manifestations of hate claimed many lives
Rape, Suicide and Murder are the tools of its destruction
I feel the pain of hate and so do you
So let's **remove the hate that lives in us**

Cocaine

I have an enemy whose name is Cocaine
He's making perfect people become insane
I knew a basketball player, who to me, was very close
He died last year of a Cocaine Overdose

Cocaine kills every minute, hour and day
I can't control this enemy; so all I do is pray
By using Cocaine once, you're caught by his hook
He's turning Lawyers and Doctors into everyday crooks

Cocaine makes the nerds think they're cool
It turns even the smartest of people into fools
People seek Cocaine because it's easy to find
Once Cocaine knows you need him, he begins to control your
mind

Cocaine tricks many into thinking that he's a friend
But one thing's for sure, **HE'LL** endure until the end
He has those, who **never** thought about death, writing their
Wills
So even the blind **can see** that Cocaine kills

Every Day Is a Good Day

No matter how many problems a day may bring
Be thankful for that day
Realize that many didn't get a chance to see it
Be thankful for that day
When we pray for Sun and get nothing but Rain
Be thankful for that day
When our bodies ache and our minds are troubled
Be thankful for that day
When we're unemployed and our bills are due
Be thankful for that day
If we are thankful for the days we **witness**
Every day is a good day!

The Darkside

I'm in my bed just staring at the ceiling
All of a sudden, I get this unexplainable feeling
A feeling of hopelessness, rejection and depression
My brain is stressed out, but my face shows no expression

I bear the ignorance of the world upon my shoulders
The conscience of the present won't wait until I'm older
Evaluate, I contemplate the thoughts I try to hide
They rule the underworld in the archives of the Darkside

Hate shall perish at the hands of its own hate
It's sad it takes an act of hate to make us all relate
Seeing sincere people blind, lost, and in the dark
Being taught the car is moving when it's still in park

Educated or Mis-Educated?
Politicians telling lies while funds are misappropriated
Release the ignorance, belligerence, and pride
They're buried deep down in the treasures of the Darkside

Don't Blow It!!!

Sunny skies and clear eyes have you mesmerized
You thought you learned in school, but you only memorized
Now you're forced to think and you can't do it
You had your 15 minutes of fame and man you blew it

From poverty to riches in 10 short years
Now your return to poverty causes your fans to shed many
tears
You had so much money you didn't know what to do
Did the people around you love your money, or did they love
you?

Most people will live a life below their financial potential
Money isn't everything, but it sure is essential
A rich man and a poor man will never financially be
comparable
Life isn't all about money, **but money sure makes life more
bearable**

THE MARK OF THE BEAST

Breathing air that's mingled with pollution
Environmental groups are starting a revolution
The "little guys" have become the major players
The "uninformed" are now focused on the Ozone Layers

Society once studied Chemistry and Biology
Now the focus is on a **"made up" Religion** called Scientology
Man has taken Scripture, polluted it – Erased it
Rhetoric is popular because **Movie Stars** have embraced it

Overweight, spoiled children are extremely lazy
Fed this madness on TV and the Internet, and we wonder why
they're CRAZY?
No longer respecting the Elders, Political Leaders and
Preachers
Fifth-Graders are now killing their Parents and shooting at
their Teachers

I can't BELIEVE what my eyes are seeing
666-Beast Monsters that used to be human-beings
The Devil is enjoying the feast
As little kids are sodomized by many of our Catholic Priests

A **mentality** of DEATH is keeping "the living" dead
We see these Beasts every day, but we're looking for the
MARKS on their Heads
Rising up, in the oven of society, like Bread and Yeast
BEWARE of the MARK OF THE BEAST!!!!

Mental Resurrection

Your body is alive but your mind is dead
Too many negative thoughts running through your head
You look to pity and sympathy for your protection
You need to rise from the ashes though **mental resurrection**

Are you tired of a vision that is totally blind?
You need to **mentally resurrect** through the RENEWING OF
YOUR MIND
Give positivity to your thoughts by removing ALL mental
pollution
Stop giving ALL of your thoughts to your problems – **focus
more on their solution**

Your mind is the FRUIT; your thoughts are the SEEDS you sow
It's your THOUGHTS that cause YOUR objects of
concentration to grow
Your THOUGHTS should be the MASTER; not the SLAVE
Mentally Resurrect your THOUGHTS to bring your mind AND
body out of the GRAVE

ME

I don't mean to sound selfish, but I need to concentrate on
ME
How I live, act, and react to society is a direct reflection of ME
I don't have time to find fault in others because I'm
constantly trying to fix ME
Self-evaluation is a full-time job that makes ME a better
person

In the past, I've been guilty of focusing on others faults
instead of focusing on ME
My faults, shortcomings and disobedience can only be
blamed on ME
My outlook on life's ups and downs can only be blamed on
ME
Life is a mirror that allows ME to see myself

When I focus on the plank in the MY eye, I'll overlook the
speck in your eye
When I concentrate on the task of resurrecting ME, I'll be
more qualified to give you life
It's not about YOU. It's ALL ABOUT ME!

God Within

I'm too busy living to be worried about dying
I'm too busy laughing to be focused on crying
I'm too busy succeeding to concentrate on failure
Positivity reigns supreme as negativity tries to assail ya

Keeping these thoughts to myself, I don't converse
I'm the God of MY TEMPLE and MY UNIVERSE
I'm the God of the Battles I've walked away from and those
I've Fought
I'm the Creator of Life and Death in ALL of my Thoughts

I'm too busy being healthy to focus on Disease
I'm too busy opening doors to EVER lose MY KEYS
I'm a God with GOD and so are YOU
Billions walk AROUND this knowledge, but those who walk
WITHIN it are few

My Reality

Analyzing my life, of 47 years, in its totality
Trying to break bread, with the dead, is my reality
Frustrated at the condition of those who have been
manipulated
A condition that **we as humans; NOT GOD**, have consistently
created

Judging one another because of the **labels** we hold
Confusing mystery with history; while believing the lies we've
been told
Concealing intentions of the heart with a deceptive face
The Un-Godly State of our Union clearly states my case

Cinderella being mistreated and sedated with chores
Wealthy Politicians and Presidents intoxicated with wars
A misinformed and uninformed society that's **trained** to be
blind
News Media and Politicians put in place to **shape our minds**

The "Golden Rule" is what I want to protect
Treating every human-being, regardless of status or title, with
the utmost respect
In my reality, actions speak louder than words
Constantly **saying, but not doing**, is totally absurd

My reality is a **World**view; not a National view
It's about Humanity as a whole; it's not just about me and
you
To achieve this reality, we must be willing to pay our dues

Are you willing to put yourself in another man or woman's shoes? **That's My Reality!**